Praise for
VALOR & VOWS

"In *Valor and Vows*, Matthew and Kristina Spencer's journey is a powerful testament to God's transformative work in marriage. Knowing them through our XO Mediation program, it's an honor to see the Spencers now thriving as they help military couples build resilient, faith-centered marriages. With personal stories, practical insights, and chapter-based discussion questions and prayers, *Valor and Vows* equips couples to navigate challenges and grow stronger together. XO Marriage is proud to be part of sharing their story with so many more."

— Brent Evans, CEO of XO Marriage

"*Valor and Vows* is an incredible resource for all military couples. Authors Matt and Kristina are the real deal and offer so much wisdom and practical steps on how to have a thriving marriage both inside and outside of military life. This resource will bless you and your marriage!"

— Dave and Ashley Willis, Marriage Coaches, Authors, Speakers, and Podcasters

"Matt and Kristina have written an insightful and biblically based guide for a successful marriage. Their shared struggles and successes bring a sense of realism to the challenges military couples face. We highly recommend this valuable work to all couples who wish to strengthen and improve their marriage."

— Dr. Steve Keith, Chaplain Colonel USAF Retired
Director Liberty University Center for Chaplains

VALOR & VOWS

Chaplain Major Matthew Spencer, USAF
& Kristina Spencer

VALOR & VOWS

A Tactical Guide to a Mission-Ready Marriage

VALOR & VOWS

VALOR & VOWS

Valor & Vows: A Tactical Guide to a Mission-Ready Marriage

Copyright © 2025 by Chaplain Major Matthew Spencer, USAF
& Kristina Spencer

ISBN: 979-8-9922693-0-7
eBook also available

Design and publishing services by wildcreativepublishing.com

valorandvows.com

Legal Disclaimer

To our beloved son, Michael. From the moment you came into our lives, we knew we wanted something greater for you—something stronger, more secure, and rooted in God's love. The covenant of our marriage holds deep meaning, not only because we love each other and God but because we want you to see the power of His grace at work in our lives.

Michael, as you know, our journey hasn't been without struggle; in fact, there were times when our marriage seemed tested beyond what we thought we could bear. But through every hardship, God showed Himself strong. Our marriage is not a story of perfection but of perseverance, faith, and transformation. It's a testimony that even in our weakest moments, God is our strength.

As you grow and one day get married, we pray that you will never give up on God and never give up on the gift of marriage. Remember, a strong marriage isn't one without challenges but one where God's love overcomes them all. We hope our journey inspires you to hold fast to faith, love, and hope, knowing that God is with you, always.

CONTENTS

INTRODUCTION

Marriage is a covenant created by God—a sacred promise that, like any military mission, requires dedication, preparation, and unwavering commitment. Yet, like so many couples, Kristina and I embarked on this journey with little understanding of the weight it carried. We came from completely different upbringings, deeply in love and ready to take on life together, yet unprepared for the unique challenges we'd face as a military couple.

I was already serving in the military when we got married, and soon after, I received orders for a year-long remote assignment. The first year of our marriage was spent apart—a reality we hadn't anticipated but one we were determined to endure. We knew marriage would be an adjustment; what we didn't realize was how testing it would be. The demands of military life only added complexity to our new roles as husband and wife.

Back in those early days, I served in security forces. I remember realizing that in all my years as a young Airman, I'd never met a chaplain or had anyone to talk to when I was struggling. During a quiet moment of reflection, I shared with Kristina, "I never had help when I was coming up in the military. If I'd had someone to talk to or guide me, maybe I wouldn't have faced so many challenges alone. What if I could be the chaplain that people actually see—someone who walks with them through the ups and downs of marriage and family life, letting them know they're not alone?" Kristina looked at me and said, "Absolutely."

As our marriage continued, so did our challenges. We struggled to prioritize each other, communicate effectively, and find a balance between our duties and our love. Eventually, we reached a point where we felt broken, on the verge of giving up. But God met us in our brokenness, showing us that if our marriage was to survive, we each had to change. Through repentance and submission, we witnessed God's hand work a miracle in our relationship.

Our journey together became the foundation for this book. In the military, every mission is guided by the commander's orders. These directives are clear, establishing structure, unity, and discipline within our teams. Even if we may not agree with every command, we follow them out of respect for the mission and for each other. Disobedience weakens the integrity of the mission and can have catastrophic consequences. The same is true in marriage. God has given us "orders" through His principles, outlining how spouses are to honor and love one another. These guidelines create stability, resilience, and a sense of purpose in our marriages, just as they do in military life.

> Genesis 2:24-25 says, "Therefore a man shall leave his father and mother and be joined to his wife, and they shall become one flesh. And they were both naked and unashamed" (NKJV).

Today, some view marriage as a social construct, something spouses can shape to fit their own preferences. Yet, when we disregard God's blueprint for marriage, we often find ourselves lost and our relationships fractured. Just as a military unit depends on a firm foundation of operational regulations to function, a marriage depends on God's principles to thrive.

For Kristina and me, understanding and applying God's guidance to our marriage brought profound change. Our story of overcoming hardship and finding healing is a testament to God's power to redeem and restore. As you walk with us through these pages, we pray you'll experience the transformative power of His love in your own marriage. With God's principles as your foundation, your marriage can be fulfilling, resilient, and joyful. You simply have to do it God's way.

Chapter 1

OATH OF OFFICE

When you became a military service member, you took an oath of office. That oath may have read something like this:

> I do solemnly swear that I will support and defend the Constitution of the United States against all enemies, foreign and domestic; that I will bear true faith and allegiance to the same; and that I will obey the orders of the President of the United States and the orders of the officers appointed over me, so help me God.

This oath signifies a commitment to honor, integrity, and public trust. It reflects a vow to maintain the highest ethical standards and uphold the values of your community, country and the agency you serve. You vow to place your service above yourself, making this oath inherently sacrificial.

Similarly, your marriage relationship must take precedence over all other priorities in your operational life. Just as you pursue growth and promotion in your military career with passion and tenacity, you must also work diligently to cultivate passion and love in your marriage. Balancing a military career with a committed marriage requires deliberate effort and strategic planning.

You put this into practice by prioritizing communication and quality time. You support each other's goals as you establish and adhere to healthy boundaries. You plan for the future, stay connected during deployments, and involve your spouse in your military life. And, when you need help, you humble yourself and ask for it.

In both your duty to country and your devotion to marriage, God calls you to operate with complete transparency and selflessness. Just as prioritizing your military calling ensures unity, safety, and mission success, prioritizing your marriage creates a secure and unified partnership.

The Bible reminds us, *"Be kindly affectionate to one another with brotherly love, in honor giving preference to one another"* (Romans 12:10, NKJV). When we honor our spouse above ourselves, we build a foundation of mutual respect and affection. This intentional choice to put each other first prevents feelings of neglect or resentment from taking root. Just as you would never leave a fellow service member behind, you're called to stand alongside your spouse, honoring and supporting them through every challenge and season.

By consistently placing each other's needs and well-being above all other earthly commitments, you build a marriage grounded in respect, affection, and unity. This kind of dedication forms a lasting bond, creating a safe and intimate relationship where both partners feel valued and loved. So set aside dedicated time for each other, maintain open communication, and protect your relationship from external pressures and distractions. Even if a marriage has faced difficulties, applying these principles can bring about positive change and transformation. We have a loving and forgiving God, and it is never too late to realign your priorities according to His design for marriage. By doing marriage God's way and placing it above all other human relationships, couples can build a strong, enduring bond that can withstand life's challenges.

DISCUSSION QUESTIONS

1. Reflect on Romans 12:10 – In what practical ways can you "give preference to one another" in your marriage? Share an example of how prioritizing your spouse's needs has strengthened your relationship. How can you implement this principle more regularly in your daily life?

2. Balancing Duty and Devotion – Military life often requires time, energy, and emotional commitment that can challenge a marriage. What are some specific ways you and your spouse can create a balance between your service duties and your relationship? How can you support each other in keeping your marriage a priority?

3. The Covenant of Marriage as a "Mission" – Just as you follow orders to accomplish a mission in the military, consider the idea of following God's principles to fulfill the "mission" of marriage. How does viewing your marriage as a mission or calling impact the way you approach challenges and difficulties? What steps can you take to protect and nurture your relationship amid life's pressures?

PRAYER

Heavenly Father, we come before You with humble hearts, grateful for the gift of marriage. Lord, help us to honor each other daily, just as You have called us to in Your Word. As Romans 12:10 says, *"Be kindly affectionate to one another with brotherly love, in honor giving preference to one another."* Teach us, Lord, to live out this verse in our marriage, always placing our spouse's needs above our own and showing kindness and respect in every word and action.

Strengthen us to navigate the unique challenges of military life with patience and grace. When the pressures of our service threaten to overwhelm us, remind us that our first earthly commitment is to each other and to the vows we made before You. Let our marriage be a place of safety, unity, and peace—a refuge from the demands of life.

Father, fill us with Your love so that we can love each other fully and selflessly. Help us to communicate openly, support each other's dreams, and find joy in every season. We trust that, with You as our foundation, our marriage can grow into a powerful testament of Your grace and faithfulness. We give You our marriage, Lord, and ask that You guide us to honor You in all that we do.

In Jesus' name, Amen.

Chapter 2
COMMS ARE ESSENTIAL

In both the military and marriage, communication is critical. I had the honor of being the Chaplain of a Combat Communications Group, and their motto was "First In, Last Out." Their mission was to establish communication networks which ensured that warfighters worldwide could stay connected as they executed their various operations. In any crisis, "comms" must be established for the team to connect to base camp. Without proper communication in battle, mission failure rates increase.

One of the most intense moments of my career came during a training exercise while I was serving in security forces. We were tasked with clearing a building when, suddenly, a gas explosion erupted. In an instant, thick smoke filled the air, obscuring our sight and disorienting our team. With vision compromised and the clock ticking, we had to rely solely on our communications equipment to navigate and clear the building.

Every word exchanged over comms took on new urgency. I had to trust that the directions I gave—and the ones I received—were precise, clear, and reliable. There was no room for misinterpretation. In that moment, I understood how vital communication is, not only to achieve our objective but to ensure the safety of every member of the team. Each command had to be concise, each response immediate. We were responsible for each other's lives, and our ability to communicate effectively became the only thing standing between us and a catastrophic outcome.

This experience reinforced the importance of preparation, trust, and teamwork. Effective communication wasn't just a tactical advantage; it was the lifeline that connected us, allowing us to move as a unit through a chaotic and dangerous situation. That day, I learned that communication isn't just about words—it's about clarity, confidence, and commitment to each other's safety. In marriage, just as in any high-stakes mission, these elements are what hold us together and enable us to navigate challenges side by side.

Husbands and wives need undisturbed face-to-face time daily to communicate. Prioritizing communication helps prevent misunderstandings and feelings of neglect. This means that friends, parents, children, and social media must remain secondary to your marriage.

Here are some tactical tips to help you approach communication with purpose and strengthen the bond with your spouse. Each of these strategies is designed to keep you both on the same page, fostering a relationship built on respect, understanding, and unwavering support.

1. Set Your Coordinates:

In the military, you wouldn't enter a mission without knowing your coordinates. Similarly, in marriage, it's essential to be clear about what you're trying to communicate and set the right "coordinates" with your partner. Take a moment to clarify your own thoughts before speaking and approach each conversation with an intentional tone, fostering a constructive and respectful exchange.

2. Keep It Mission-Focused:

Just as military orders must be focused and relevant, conversations in marriage should stay mission-focused—addressing the issue directly without detouring into unrelated frustrations or emotions. Staying on-topic and respecting each other's time ensures you both feel heard and prevents additional misunderstandings. Remember, you're not opposing each other; you're working together as a team to overcome a challenge.

3. Check Your Integrity Levels:

Military communication relies on accuracy and integrity, where the information given is honest and reliable. In marriage, being truthful and open about your feelings, needs, and expectations creates a strong foundation of trust. Even if it's difficult, share honestly to avoid misunderstandings and build confidence in one another.

4. Establish a Safe Zone:

Security is vital in the field, and in marriage, creating a "safe zone" for communication is equally important. Ensure that each partner feels comfortable sharing openly without fear of judgment or reaction. This safe environment promotes vulnerability and intimacy, deepening your connection.

5. Request and Respond to Feedback:

Feedback in military operations allows for real-time course corrections. In marriage, listening actively and asking for your partner's perspective strengthens teamwork. By regularly checking in with each other and validating each other's feelings, you create a balanced approach that promotes growth and understanding.

This hits close to home for me. For years, the challenge wasn't what Kristina was trying to communicate, but how she was communicating it. The moment I sensed a shift in her approach, I would instantly shut down. I remember a particularly revealing moment during counseling when Kristina said something that made me withdraw immediately. Our counselor pointed out, "Just because what you say is true does not mean it is kind." That advice struck a chord.

The next morning, which happened to be the 31st of the month, Kristina came across Proverbs 31:26: "She opens her mouth with wisdom, and on her tongue is the law of kindness" (NKJV). This verse was a turning point for her. She realized that if our marriage was to improve, the way she spoke to me needed to change. In our next counseling session, I was able to articulate to her, "You can tell me anything, in the right tone." To me, tone mattered more than anything else.

This simple but profound shift became a cornerstone in our journey toward a healthier, more loving marriage. Kristina's commitment to speaking with kindness and wisdom, coupled with my openness to listen without defensiveness, allowed us to rebuild trust and strengthen our connection. We both began to see that true communication isn't just about expressing our thoughts but doing so in a way that honors each other's hearts. Proverbs 31:26 became a guiding light, reminding us that words spoken with love and respect have the power to heal, uplift, and transform.

From that day on, we committed to making our words a source of strength and unity, building a marriage where love and kindness lead the way.

DISCUSSION QUESTIONS

I. **Reflect on Proverbs 31:26** – In what ways can you practice "speaking with wisdom and kindness" in your marriage? How might shifting the tone of your words impact your partner's ability to feel heard and valued?

2. **The Importance of How You Communicate**– Think about a time when how you communicated affected a conversation with your spouse, either positively or negatively. How did it shape the outcome of the conversation? How can you be more intentional about your tone to foster openness and understanding?

3. **Turning Points in Communication** – This story highlights a turning point where a simple shift in communication led to deeper respect and connection. Are there areas in your own relationship where changing your communication style could lead to a positive turning point? What practical steps can you take to achieve this?

PRAYER

Heavenly Father, we come before You with grateful hearts, recognizing that You are the foundation of our marriage. Lord, remind us daily that we are not adversaries but partners, called to face life's challenges together as a team. Help us to see each other with eyes of compassion, to communicate with kindness, and to seek solutions that bring us closer rather than apart.

Grant us wisdom to understand one another deeply, patience to listen fully, and humility to put each other's needs before our own. When disagreements arise, let us approach them with grace, remembering that our love is stronger than any conflict. Strengthen our bond, Lord, and help us to honor You by honoring each other.

Thank You for guiding us and for being our source of strength. May Your love and peace fill our home, and may we continually build each other up as we walk this journey together. In Jesus' name, we pray, Amen.

Chapter 3
MISSION ESSENTIAL

Anyone who knows me knows that I'm an avid outdoorsman. Hunting and fishing are more than hobbies to me; they're part of who I am. For as long as I can remember, I've spent countless hours in nature, captivated by its sights, sounds, and wonders. When Kristina and I first got married, I made it clear that I would continue pursuing my passions, regardless of her feelings on the matter. In a single year, I'd easily spend around 60 days on hunting and fishing trips, while Kristina and I only managed about 10 days of vacation together.

As you can imagine, this wasn't a strategy for unity or peace in our home. Over time, Kristina's initial anger turned into indifference. Our communication broke down, and our intimacy faded. To make things even more complicated, I was also prioritizing my family of origin above my marriage, which I assumed was normal due to my close-knit upbringing. But Kristina felt like she was in a losing competition for my attention.

It took a counseling session for me to realize that our marriage needed a shift in perspective. My counselor challenged me to approach my relationship with Kristina with the same mission-essential mindset that I bring to my work in the military. When I started viewing our marriage as mission essential, I understood that our union wasn't just a personal relationship—it was a purposeful one, designed by God to impact not only our lives but also those of future generations.

In the military, we know the importance of focusing on mission-critical tasks, and marriage, especially in a military life, is no different. A healthy, resilient marriage creates a ripple effect that extends far beyond our own lives. When we make our marriage mission essential, we set a powerful example for future generations. Ecclesiastes 4:9-12 reminds us, *"Two are better than one, because they have a good return for their labor: If either of them falls down, one can help the other up...Though one may be overpowered, two can defend themselves. A cord of three strands is not quickly broken"* (NIV).

This commitment impacts everything. A strong marriage reduces stress, increases productivity, and positively influences the broader mission. Spouses who are emotionally supported and secure at home are better equipped to handle the demands of military life, and the effects of a healthy marriage extend to our children, who grow up feeling safe and grounded. Studies have shown that children from stable homes perform better in school, are more resilient, and often go on to lead lives of purpose and success. This ripple effect strengthens not only our family but also the communities and economies we're part of, ultimately enhancing the mission. In contrast, the domino effect of a struggling marriage or divorce can be devastating. The personal cost is high, with stress levels and mental health challenges rising. Productivity suffers, and the mission can be compromised. Children from broken homes often face additional struggles, impacting their performance in school and their own relationships. When marriages falter, the effects are felt across every area of life, ultimately weakening the very fabric of the family and the community.

Seeing our marriage as mission essential means committing to each other with intentionality and purpose. It means understanding that our union has a purpose bigger than ourselves. In this mindset, Kristina and I are called to make our marriage a priority, recognizing that each time we invest in it, we're creating a legacy of strength, resilience, and faithfulness. We establish our marriage as a stronghold, capable of withstanding the challenges of life and military demands alike. And as we live this out, we hope to inspire others to see their marriages as mission essential too—a powerful foundation that supports them and enables them to make an impact in their own lives and communities.

My love for hunting and fishing is still there, but my priorities have shifted. I've come to enjoy these pursuits without guilt because I know that Kristina and I are in this together, sharing experiences that strengthen our bond. When I place my marriage first, I gain so much more—a strong partnership that enriches my life, supports our mission, and creates a lasting legacy for future generations.

DISCUSSION QUESTIONS

1. **The Mission of Marriage** – Reflect on the idea of marriage as "mission essential." How might viewing your relationship with your spouse as a purposeful, mission-critical partnership change the way you approach challenges? What intentional steps can you take to protect and prioritize this mission?

2. **The Domino Effect** – Consider the ripple effects of a strong, healthy marriage versus a struggling one. In what ways do you see your own marriage impacting your family, your career, and the community around you? How can investing in your marriage create positive outcomes for those who follow in your footsteps?

3. Leaving a Legacy – A mission-essential marriage builds a legacy for future generations. What values, habits, or examples would you like to pass down to your children or others looking to you for guidance? How can you model a marriage that reflects resilience, unity, and purpose?

PRAYER

Heavenly Father, we come before You with humble hearts, grateful for the sacred gift of marriage. Thank You for the purpose You have woven into our union, a purpose that extends beyond ourselves and into the lives of future generations. Lord, help us to see our marriage as mission essential, as a foundation that strengthens us, our family, and our community.

We ask for Your guidance in prioritizing each other above all earthly relationships, seeking unity, and building a bond that can withstand every challenge. Teach us to communicate with love, to serve each other selflessly, and to honor You in all we do. Let our marriage reflect Your grace and goodness, showing others the beauty of a partnership rooted in faith.

Lord, we pray for the strength to lead by example, that our commitment to one another may create a legacy of love, resilience, and faithfulness. May our children and those around us see the impact of a marriage built on Your principles and be inspired to seek the same. Father, protect our union, guard our hearts, and help us to keep our eyes fixed on You as the ultimate source of our strength.

Thank You for being with us on this journey. We trust in Your faithfulness, knowing that with You at the center, our marriage will stand firm. In Jesus' name, we pray. Amen.

Chapter 4
ENDURING MISSION
Love For the Long Haul

Prioritizing romance can seem daunting amidst the challenges of long hours, extended deployments, and lengthy times away from loved ones. yet it's both possible and essential. The strength of a romantic relationship can serve as a steadfast anchor, providing emotional resilience and a sense of home even when you're many miles away. Obviously, physical intimacy is a very important part of a marriage, but what do you do when you and your spouse are apart? It's time to realize that love is so much more than sex.

> "[Love] bears all things, believes all things, hopes all things, endures all things. Love never fails." 1 Corinthians 13:7-8 NKJV

As we mentioned earlier, the first year of our marriage, Kristina and I lived apart. I was on a remote assignment in Korea, and she was in the US living with our family. I remember that year being one of the most challenging of my career. I had been in the Air Force for roughly three years, my vocation was stressful, and I had never been that far from home. Kristina and I had just gotten married and were not able to live together. We had to face the normal challenges of being a newlywed couple while also dealing with a literal distance of thousands of miles.

If we were going to communicate, we had to write letters and purchase calling cards to use with landline telephones.

Modern technology has made things more manageable these days with video calls, instant messaging, and social media. These tools better enable couples to share moments of their day, express their feelings, and stay updated on each other's lives. But it doesn't happen automatically. Both spouses must dedicate time for these interactions and treating them as non-negotiable appointments.

Understanding and empathy also play significant roles in nurturing romance. Military life comes with unique stresses, and it's essential to acknowledge and respect each other's experiences and emotions. The service member must recognize the challenges their partner faces in their absence, such as handling the household, caring for children, or simply dealing with loneliness. Similarly, the non-service partner must recognize the pressures and dangers of military service. Support and encouragement have to go both ways.

When Kristina and I would talk during our time apart, I had to be mindful of her stresses as she needed to be empathetic to mine. I felt as if life around me was constantly evolving, yet my personal world had stood still. Receiving pictures from my wife was both heart-warming and depressing; my heart leaped every time I saw her face, but it crushed me to see how much things in back home were changing. Kristina felt the stress of maintaining our household when we did not have a home, and there was a constant sense of displacement because all of our belongings were in boxes.

Surprises and small gestures go a long way in keeping romance alive. A handwritten letter, a flower delivery, a care package, or a small gift can speak volumes about your love and dedication. These acts show that despite the distance and demanding nature of military life, your partner is always on your mind. A little bit of planning, even for a virtual moment, can go a long way in keeping the spark alive.

Time together is precious, and making the most of it is vital. When you're on leave, prioritize your partner and make every moment count. Plan activities you both enjoy, have deep conversations, and reconnect on every level. While family, children, and friends can be demanding, carve out non-negotiable time for you and your spouse to reconnect. These moments are the building blocks of your relationship because they create memories that can be cherished and leaned on during times apart.

Moreover, a support network can significantly impact your relationship's health. This includes other military families who understand your unique challenges and can offer support and advice. Engaging in community activities or support groups can provide both partners with a sense of belonging and understanding. This can help ease the strains that military life tends to impose on marriages. Some of the most impactful relationships Kristina and I have come from our military brothers and sisters. I'll never forget the time I was away and Kristina became so sick that she could not take care of herself or our son. Her military sisters immediately stepped up and provided the round-the-clock care she needed to recover. I cannot encourage you enough to make the most of your military family opportunities by getting involved in squadron events, spouses clubs, chapel functions, etc.

For many couples, a shared belief system (faith) provides strength and guidance. Praying together, sharing spiritual thoughts, or participating in faith-based activities can offer comfort and reinforce your commitment to each other. It's also important to acknowledge and address any struggles. Don't be scared to seek help when needed, whether through counseling, connecting with your Chaplain or support groups, or talking to trusted friends or mentors. Addressing issues head-on rather than letting them fester prevents small problems from morphing into insurmountable barriers.

DISCUSSION QUESTIONS

1. **Prioritizing Connection** – In the busyness of military life, it's easy for romance to take a back seat. What are some intentional ways you and your spouse can prioritize time together, even during demanding seasons? How does making time for each other strengthen your bond?

2. **Staying Emotionally Engaged** – Long distances, deployments, and constant moves can create emotional distance in a relationship. How can you work to maintain emotional intimacy, even when you're apart? What are some creative ways to express love and appreciation from afar?

3. **Building a Lasting Love** – Reflect on the idea of "mission love for the long haul." What values or habits do you believe are essential for a love that endures? How can you continue to nurture romance and affection throughout different stages of your marriage?

PRAYER

Heavenly Father, we thank You for the gift of love and the beauty of marriage. In a life filled with unique challenges and uncertainties, we ask for Your guidance and strength to keep our love vibrant and enduring. Teach us to cherish each other deeply, to nurture our connection even when circumstances pull us apart, and to always seek ways to show love and appreciation for one another.

Lord, help us to prioritize our marriage, making time for moments of joy, laughter, and intimacy. When distance separates us, let our hearts remain close and our love unwavering. Remind us that romance is not just in grand gestures but in the simple, everyday acts of kindness, thoughtfulness, and devotion.

Father, give us creativity and wisdom to express our love in ways that build a lasting bond. May we stay rooted in faith, leaning on Your strength to sustain us and fill our hearts with passion and commitment for each other. Let our marriage reflect Your love, becoming a source of inspiration and hope to those around us.

We entrust our relationship to You, Lord, knowing that with You at the center, our love will endure for the long haul. In Jesus' name, we pray. Amen.

Chapter 5
TACTICAL ENGAGEMENT

One of my bucket list goals was to compete in a fitness competition. To achieve it, I needed a solid action plan and a lot of discipline. I had to overhaul my everyday routine to fit in twice-daily workouts, completely revamp my diet, and stay consistent with my regimen. The process was intense and lasted about six months, but the day of the competition finally arrived, and I was thrilled to win. It was the daily effort, mental preparation, and relentless dedication that got me there.

The same idea applies to your relationship with your spouse: you will only succeed in marriage if you put in the effort. This means paying attention to what your spouse needs or wants, even if it's different from what you need or want. Kristina and I are often asked how to balance pursuing your spouse with the demands of military service. I remember a time when I was assigned to work on Air Force One detail. It was a huge honor, but it came with the challenge of being on call 24/7, especially during an election year with frequent presidential visits. My schedule was demanding, and it caused a lot of stress in our marriage.

To help our relationship stay strong, Kristina and I had to be proactive, and with limited funds, we had to get creative. At night, we would put our son to bed, bake cookies, and spend a few moments enjoying each other's company. We made it a rule not to talk about work, money, or our son during these times. Sometimes it was tough to find other things to talk about, so we came up with a list of topics. Did the conversation always flow naturally? No, but we kept putting in the effort to communicate to the best of our abilities.

During a rough patch when we were in constructive separation and going through XO Mediation, Kristina went above and beyond. She drove three hours each week to clean the house, do laundry, iron my uniforms, and prepare my meals because she knew my schedule was overwhelming. Even though our marriage was on the rocks and I wasn't interested in working on it, Kristina never kept score or asked for anything in return. Her unconditional love and support softened my heart and made me fall in love with her all over again. Over time, our marriage healed.

One piece of advice we received years ago sticks with me: "Give what you want, and you will get what you need." Serving your spouse without expecting anything in return is similar to the selflessness we show our partners, battle buddies, or wingmen. When you approach your marriage with this mindset, you end up fulfilled and connected in ways you never thought possible.

Song of Solomon 2:16 says, "My beloved is mine, and I am his; he browses among the lilies" (NIV). Kristina absolutely loves this verse because it captures the essence of mutual belonging and continuous pursuit that should define a marriage. It highlights the importance of viewing your spouse as a cherished partner, bound together in a loving and committed relationship. The imagery of tending to the lilies represents the ongoing, tender care and pursuit of one another, perfectly aligning with the idea of nurturing and prioritizing your marriage.

DISCUSSION QUESTIONS

1. How can we actively pursue each other while dealing with the shifting demands of military life?

2. What are some specific actions or habits we can develop to help each other feel loved and pursued, even when physically apart?

3. How do you feel when I make an intentional effort to pursue you? How can we maintain that feeling during challenging seasons?

PRAYER

Heavenly Father, we thank You for the gift of marriage and the privilege of walking through life together. As we seek to engage with each other more intentionally, we ask for Your guidance to help us approach our relationship with purpose and care. Show us how to love each other strategically, always considering each other's needs and serving one another with humility and devotion.

Lord, remind us of the words in Song of Solomon 2:16: "My beloved is mine, and I am his." May this truth be a foundation in our hearts, strengthening our bond and reminding us that we belong to each other. Help us to communicate openly, listen intently, and support each other through every challenge, cherishing the gift of being fully known and fully loved.

Teach us to be mindful of our words and actions, knowing that each one has the power to build up or tear down. Give us wisdom in how we approach each other, courage to address difficult issues, and patience to grow through them together.

Strengthen us, Father, so that we may stand united against any obstacle, ready to face life's battles side by side. Equip us with Your love and grace, and help us to see our marriage as a powerful partnership—a mission where we're called to support, uplift, and cherish each other. May we always be reminded that, with You at the center, we have everything we need to engage with purpose and achieve a relationship that honors You.

In Jesus' name, we pray. Amen.

Chapter 6

CHAIN OF COMMAND

God's Plan for Marriage

One of my most interesting moments in counseling is when we talk about the roles of husbands and wives in marriage. Almost instantly, I can see awkward shifting in seats and eyes rolling. Ephesians 5:22–24 emphasizes the role of wives, instructing them to submit to their husbands as they do to the Lord. This submission is not about inferiority but about respecting and supporting the husband's leadership. Similarly, in the military, we have a chain of command. The respect we show our chain of command is not a sign of weakness but a recognition of the structured hierarchy essential for operational efficiency and success. Just as a soldier trusts this commander's decisions for the greater mission, a wife's respect and trust in her husband's leadership contribute to the harmony and purpose of the marriage.

In verses 25–28, the apostle Paul commands husbands to love their wives, "just as Christ loved the church and gave himself up for her" (NIV). This sacrificial love requires husbands to prioritize their wives' well-being above their own, while demonstrating a servant-leader approach. In the military, leaders are expected to care for their troops, often putting their soldiers'' needs ahead of their own. A good military leader ensures that their soldiers are well-prepared, protected, and supported, even at the cost of personal sacrifice. This servant leadership is crucial for maintaining the morale and effectiveness of a unit, much like how a husband's loving leadership strengthens the marital bond.

For husbands, this is the greatest call to leadership and an awesome privilege. Think of it this way: Jesus is our Commander in Chief, and we as husbands are the Vice President. The closer we are to Jesus, the easier it is for us to hear Him cast the vision for our marriages, children, finances, future, homes, and more. From there, we can properly cast that vision to our wives, and then as a team, we can execute that vision for our family. The more we love Jesus, the more we are able to love our wives because He reveals them to us in a unique and special way. He understands them better than we do. He knows the weight of the burdens they carry more than we do. When we remain close to Him in our daily relationship, He leads and guides us on how to strengthen our relationship with them.

The concept of mutual respect and responsibility in Ephesians 5 aligns so well with our military culture because it reminds us that every role, from the highest-ranking officer to the lowest-ranking soldier, is vital. Each member of the military must understand their position and duties, just as husbands and wives must understand and respect their roles within the marriage. This mutual respect fosters a cohesive and effective team, whether on the battlefield or within the household.

Ephesians 5:31 speaks to the unity in marriage, where two become one flesh. This unity is akin to the camaraderie and brotherhood found in the military. Soldiers train together, fight together, and often live together, creating a bond that transcends individual differences. This unity is critical for mission success, much like the oneness in marriage is vital for a strong and enduring relationship.

The parallel between Ephesians 5 and the military chain of command also underscores the importance of effective communication and accountability. In the military, communication and accountability ensure that orders are understood and executed correctly, preventing chaos and confusion. Similarly, in marriage, communication between spouses builds understanding, trust, and cooperation. Accountability in fulfilling each other's needs and responsibilities strengthens the marital bond and prevents misunderstandings.

In both contexts, the ultimate goal is to achieve a greater purpose. For the military, it's the successful completion of missions and the protection of national interests. For marriage, it's the creation of a loving, supportive partnership that reflects God's love and purpose. Both require commitment, sacrifice, and a willingness to put the other first.

Ephesians 5 and the military chain of command both emphasize structured leadership, mutual respect, sacrificial love, and unity. By embracing these values, whether in uniform or in the sacred bond of marriage, we can fulfill our God-given roles and responsibilities, leading to a more harmonious and purposeful life.

DISCUSSION QUESTIONS

1. How do we see the idea of "chain of command" applying to our marriage, and what does it look like when we honor God as our ultimate authority within our relationship?

2. In what ways can we practice mutual submission and respect, while also embracing the different roles we each play in our marriage?

3. How do we handle times when one of us needs to take the lead in decision-making, and how can we ensure that leadership is rooted in love and unity?

PRAYER

Heavenly Father, we thank You for the blessing of marriage and the order You designed for our relationships. Help us to understand and embrace the concept of a "chain of command" in our lives, with You as our ultimate guide and foundation. Teach us to place our marriage at the top of our priorities, knowing that this commitment strengthens not only our union but also our family and the communities we serve.

Lord, grant us wisdom to honor each other daily, to respect one another's roles, and to work together as a united team. May we seek to serve each other in humility, placing each other's needs above our own. Show us how to prioritize our relationship in the decisions we make, protecting it with the same diligence we bring to our other responsibilities.

When distractions arise, help us to stay focused on each other, building a relationship that honors You and reflects Your love. May our marriage be an example of strength, respect, and unity—a partnership that brings You glory and inspires those around us. Guide us to follow Your lead as we strive to love, serve, and uplift one another every day.

In Jesus' name, we pray. Amen.

Chapter 7
SERVICE BEFORE SELF

There is a four-letter word that best describes what it takes to have a successful marriage: WORK! It makes me smile when Kristina and I have counseling sessions with couples who say, "We want a marriage like yours." What they see is the end result of a lot of surrender, sacrifice, and work. There is a misconception that working at a marriage means you don't have a good marriage. That is so far from the truth. The reality is anything worth having in life comes from a solid work ethic.

In the military, namely the Air Force, one of our core values is "Service before Self." This core value underscores the commitment to the mission, unit, and country above personal interests. It is integral to maintaining the discipline, cohesion, and effectiveness of military operations. We swear fidelity and loyalty to our military service, and we need to swear the same fidelity and loyalty to our marriage.

This idea resonates deeply with the teaching found in 1 Corinthians 13, where Paul describes the essence of love as patient, kind, and selfless. He writes, *"Love does not seek its own"* (1 Corinthians 13:5, NKJV), reminding us that genuine love looks beyond personal desires and focuses on the needs of others. This kind of love demands selflessness and a willingness to put another person's well-being first, just as we do in our service to our country.

Paul's words challenge us to live out sacrificial love in our relationships, especially in marriage. True love is not self-centered; it's a daily choice to serve, uplift, and support our spouse, even when it's challenging. Paul's description of love as *"bearing all things, believing all things, hoping all things, enduring all things"* (1 Corinthians 13:7, NKJV) captures the essence of sacrificial love—a love that endures hardship, forgives freely, and remains steadfast. When we choose to put our spouse first, we build a marriage rooted in service, humility, and strength, creating a bond that can weather any storm.

Just as we commit wholeheartedly to our mission and our teammates, we are called to dedicate ourselves fully to our spouse. In marriage, embodying sacrificial love means reflecting Christ's love through our actions. Prioritizing our spouse's needs creates a relationship that honors God and builds a love that endures. By choosing to serve our spouse each day, we cultivate a partnership grounded in peace, unity, and shared purpose.

In the military, the mission always comes first, and values like unit cohesion, sacrifice, discipline, and training follow. These principles, along with leadership by example, ethical standards, and a commitment to excellence, honor, loyalty, and respect, are not only essential for our service—they're essential for a thriving marriage. In a military marriage, just as in our work, it's important to embrace discipline and training. By investing in our relationship, communicating openly, and setting aside time to connect, we stay resilient and united, even amid life's challenges. Leading by example also matters; when we demonstrate respect, love, and commitment, we inspire our spouse to reflect those values back to us, strengthening our bond.

Sacrifice, too, is at the heart of both military service and marriage. Sacrificial love doesn't always require grand gestures; it's often found in small, meaningful acts of care and thoughtfulness. Showing your spouse they're a priority can be as simple as sharing a text of encouragement, or sending a funny dad joke to brighten their day. One day, Kristina looked at me with a playful smile and said, "Sweetheart, you know it's biblical for the man to make the coffee every morning." I raised an eyebrow and asked, "Oh really? Where does it say that?" With a grin, she replied, "Hebrews." The joke made us both laugh, but it also got me thinking. I decided to start making coffee for her each morning as a small act of service. It's something she truly appreciates, especially since her morning routine is one of the most important parts of her day. This simple gesture has become a way to show her that I'm thinking of her needs and that she's a priority to me. In turn, she ensures my uniforms are prepped and ready each day. This act of kindness means so much to me because it allows me to put my best foot forward, and it shows me how deeply she supports the calling God has given me. Knowing she takes care of this for me is a constant reminder of her love and commitment to our shared mission. When we live out this kind of love daily—choosing small ways to serve, encourage, and uplift—we build a marriage that endures, honors our commitment, and stands as a testament to God's love.

We had a pastor and his wife tell us years ago to become lifelong learners of one another. Take assessments on your spouse's needs and do your best to meet those needs. Work as a team, pull together, and cover one another, as you would your soldiers in arms. Give what you want, and you will get what you need.

The values that drive us in the military—service before self, discipline, ethical standards, and sacrifice—are the same values that can lead to a successful and fulfilling marriage. By embracing these principles and working diligently on our relationships, we can create marriages that not only survive but also thrive.

DISCUSSION QUESTIONS

1. How can we better practice "service before self" in our marriage, ensuring that we prioritize each other's needs and well-being above our own?

2. How can we serve each other in our daily lives in ways that reflect Christ's example of selflessness, especially during challenging deployment seasons or high-stress situations?

3. How do we find a balance between serving each other selflessly and making sure we also take care of ourselves, both physically and emotionally?

PRAYER

Heavenly Father, we thank You for the gift of marriage and the joy of serving one another. Help us to recognize the significance of the small, everyday acts of kindness that strengthen our bond and remind us of Your love. Teach us to see these gestures as expressions of our commitment, love, and support for one another.

Lord, may we continue to look for ways to bless each other through simple acts of service. Let these actions speak volumes, showing our gratitude for each other and our dedication to the calling You have placed on our lives. As we serve one another, may we grow closer to You, reflecting Your heart in our marriage.

Guide us, Father, to cherish and support one another in ways that uplift, encourage, and honor the love we share. May our marriage be a testament to Your faithfulness, filled with love that serves and strengthens daily. In Jesus' name, we pray. Amen.

Chapter 8
MISSION FOCUSED

Kristina and I once found ourselves on the brink of divorce. We knew that God had brought us together, but we couldn't understand why. During a season of fasting and prayer, the Lord revealed what we believe is our divine purpose in both marriage and ministry: to build the temple, feed the orphans, and season the people. This calling led us beyond the comfort of the pulpit and into the lives of those we're called to serve. Too often, ministry stays within the four walls because that feels safe, but God was urging us toward a more hands-on, tactical approach in both our ministry and our marriage.

Proverbs 29:18 tells us, *"Where there is no vision, the people perish"* (KJ21). Vision provides the clear direction needed for growth and unity, offering both motivation and momentum for you and your spouse. Just as an archer takes aim with a focused eye on the target, vision in marriage sets the course and aligns every action toward a shared purpose. Without vision, a marriage can drift, eventually deteriorating. Just as commanders cast vision for their units and plan for execution, we must cast vision for our marriages, setting clear goals and establishing systems to reach them. It's often said, *"If you fail to plan, you plan to fail."* Goals define the results you want, but it's the systems—the practical steps and daily disciplines—that will ultimately help you achieve them. In other words, we don't rise to the level of our goals; we fall to the level of our systems.

Take time together to develop a clear vision for your marriage and family. Think of it as a staff meeting where you align on the weekly, monthly, and even yearly vision and set the action plans that will bring it to life. Kristina and I hold regular "vision meetings" for our marriage, where we discuss essential topics like finances, children, vacations, and even romance. We keep these meetings short and focused, usually 15-20 minutes, especially when covering more logical topics like finances. Having a written agenda keeps us on track, helps us stay logical, and allows us to hold each other accountable to the goals we set together. We find that structuring these meetings monthly, quarterly, semi-annually, and annually helps us stay aligned as we pursue our shared vision.

This will keep your marriage on target, providing direction and a sense of unity. Without it, deterioration is inevitable. Habakkuk 2:2 reminds us, *"Write the vision, and make it plain."* When you write down your vision and keep it at the forefront, it becomes something you can aim for and, with God's help, bring into reality. Setting a clear vision and actionable plans will guide your marriage and help you fulfill the purpose God has set for you. By taking this approach, you can build a strong, unified marriage that reflects God's love and purpose.

A strong marriage with vision is like a well-aimed arrow, steady and sure, capable of impacting generations to come. Keep your vision at the forefront, review it often, and let it guide every decision. Just as I aim carefully in archery, let each of us approach our marriage with intention, hitting the mark that God has set before us.

DISCUSSION QUESTIONS

1. How can we stay mission-focused in our marriage, ensuring that our relationship remains a top priority even as we balance the demands of military life?

2. In what ways can we view our marriage as a mission God has given us, and how can we work together to fulfill that mission?

3. When challenges arise in our marriage, how can we adopt a mission-focused mindset to overcome obstacles and achieve success together?

PRAYER

Heavenly Father, we come before You with grateful hearts, acknowledging that You are the source of all wisdom and purpose. We ask for Your guidance as we seek to build a vision for our marriage and family—a vision that aligns with Your will and reflects Your love. Lord, plant in our hearts a clear direction for our lives together, one that honors You and draws us closer to each other and to the purpose You've set before us.

Your Word says in Proverbs, *"Where there is no vision, the people perish."* Help us to see clearly, Father, to set our sights on a purpose that brings life, unity, and hope. Let Your Spirit guide us as we develop our goals and plan the steps needed to achieve them. Show us how to make our vision a priority, to keep it alive and at the forefront of our minds, especially when distractions and challenges arise.

Lord, give us the courage to pursue our vision with faith, perseverance, and humility. May our commitment to this vision become a foundation of strength in our marriage, a guide for every decision, and a source of inspiration to those around us.

Help us to remain focused on the calling You've placed on our lives, trusting that as we seek Your will, You will provide the wisdom, direction, and strength we need to fulfill it.

Thank You, Lord, for Your faithfulness and for the privilege of walking this journey together. In Jesus' name, we pray. Amen.

Chapter 9
WATCH MY SIX

It is believed that the term "Watch my six" originated during World War I. In those analog days, pilots referred to the front of the plane as their twelve o'clock, making the rear of the plane their six. When one pilot would tell another to "Watch my six" or "Cover my six," they were asking their wingman to protect them from enemy fire. This relationship was a cohesive unit built on a foundation of trust unlike any other. They knew beyond a shadow of a doubt that they had each other's back.

2001 changed my life forever, as it did for so many Americans. I had been enlisted for a little over a year, working in the missile field and running nuclear convoys. I was on a routine "trip," as we called it, but this one would change the course of my career forever.

The guys and I always planned an outing after each trip to the field, and this time was no exception. Bags packed, elk tags in hand, it was our favorite time of year. Early September in the Rockies is a spectacular time for an outdoorsman. However, planes hit the Twin Towers that day, Americans perished, and as I arrived to do the changeover on base, my team and I were instructed to keep our weapons and go back to the field. We didn't know for how long; we just knew that America was under attack, Threatcon Delta was in place, and we were at war. As a nuclear missile cop, the possibility of us engaging in nuclear warfare became very real. To say we were stunned, somber, and scared would be an understatement. When I enlisted, I never fully comprehended that I might actually have to go to war.

All the training I had learned now had to be put into practice. There was no time for a refresher or a check-up. This was real. There was a moment while watching footage of the planes hitting the towers when we all looked at one another. No words were said, but instinctively, we knew we would "Cover each other's six." Looking back, I couldn't have picked a better team of young men to face whatever was ahead of us. We trained together and knew each other's strengths and weaknesses. Where one needed support, another gave it. We didn't have time to complain or pick at each other. The magnitude of the evil was real, but we were committed to fight for one another and for our freedom. We pulled together, knowing the mission in front of us was greater than ourselves. It drove us and gave us the strength to accomplish our goal.

God designed marriage to work much the same way. Two become one. "Mine" becomes "ours." It goes way beyond sex into a much deeper level of intimacy. Kristina and I have learned over the years that we are each other's wingman. In moments of frustration, Kristina reminds me, "I am on your team." Knowing that I have someone on my side whom I can rely on is such a comfort to me. She has become my best friend—my ride or die. We are in this together, no matter what.

Just like in the military, the strength of our partnership lies in our commitment to cover each other's six. We trust each other implicitly, and this trust is the foundation of our marriage. We understand that our mission is greater than ourselves, and this understanding gives us the motivation and strength to work together, fight for each other, and build a marriage that reflects God's love and purpose.

DISCUSSION QUESTIONS

1. How can we better watch each other's six in our marriage, ensuring that we are always protecting and supporting each other in the face of life's challenges?

2. What are some practical ways we can watch each other's six during times of separation, such as deployments or training, to ensure that our connection remains strong?

3. How do we communicate when we feel like our six isn't being watched, and how can we address those moments with grace and understanding?

PRAYER

Heavenly Father, we come before You with gratitude for the gift of marriage and the honor of standing beside one another in this life. Lord, we ask for Your strength and guidance as we commit to "watch each other's six"—to protect, support, and encourage one another through every season.

Teach us to be vigilant, always aware of our spouse's needs and willing to stand in the gap for each other. When one of us feels weak, remind us to be a source of strength; when one of us feels uncertain, may we bring reassurance and courage. Help us to guard each other's hearts, to speak words that uplift, and to act with love and loyalty. Just as a soldier trusts their partner in the field, may we trust each other deeply, knowing that we are never alone.

Lord, give us the wisdom to recognize threats to our relationship—whether they come from within or from outside influences. May we be quick to listen, slow to speak, and eager to seek Your guidance when challenges arise. Help us to build a bond so strong that it withstands every trial, with You as our ultimate protector and guide.

Father, we ask that You surround our marriage with Your divine protection. May we always be united, watching out for each other's well-being, and carrying one another's burdens. Strengthen our love, deepen our trust, and grant us the resilience to face each day with confidence, knowing that together, with You at the center, we can overcome anything.

In Jesus' name, we pray. Amen.

Chapter 10
TOP COVER

In military combat, the concept of "cover" refers to anything that can physically protect an individual from enemy fire. Providing "top cover" involves using aircraft to provide aerial protection for ground forces against enemy attacks. When ground troops are engaged in a difficult operation, aircraft fly above to ensure their safety. If the enemy attacks, the aircraft fire on the enemy to protect their soldiers.

I speak with Airmen every day, and one topic that consistently comes up is leadership. I hear it discussed from both vantage points. On one hand, I hear about immediate supervisors or senior leaders who leave their team hanging when backed against a wall or abuse their authority and exhibit a pattern of dominance. On the other hand, I hear praise for immediate supervisors or senior leaders who provide excellent top cover. The quality and success of the team are measured by a leader's ability to provide that top cover. Research supports this not only in the military but also in corporate structures. Exceptional leaders support, protect, and provide top cover for their team. Because the team feels valued and part of something greater than themselves, they rise to any challenge. Leaders cast vision, and the team executes that vision with excellence. When the team feels protected, supported, and provided for, they grow and develop.

In our lives and marriages, Jesus provides that top cover. He ensures we are provided for, protected, and loved sacrificially. He bore the burden of our sin and shame. When we are backed against a wall, He never leaves us hanging. He never passes the buck, plays the blame game, exerts dominance, or makes excuses.

For years, Kristina and I failed as a team. Don't get me wrong—we worked very hard, but we worked incorrectly. We worked individually instead of collectively. We worked against the grain instead of with it. I would go one way; she would go another. We did not communicate. I would make decisions regarding finances or how to spend my time, and she did the same. Then something would come up, and we realized we double-booked or double-spent, causing great tension and stress, which could have been avoided if we had communicated and worked as a team from the beginning. She dominated me with her tone and anger, and I dominated her by stonewalling. As a leader, I did not provide the top cover I should have. I left her hanging out to dry. I blamed and pointed the finger. She would also acknowledge that when I did try to provide the proper top cover, she did not support me. Trust was broken, and our team was fractured.

We finally both acknowledged that we needed Jesus to come in and be the top cover for us, and when we vowed to stay under His cover, our marriage changed. I began to make the daily decision to lead, and she made the daily decision to be led. It was not easy at first. You don't always get ahead right away by providing top cover, whether on the job or as the head of your home. There is still an enemy working diligently to get in between you and your spouse. It is consistency in providing top cover and leading with a servant's heart that enables you to live victoriously. I had to be consistent in my actions for trust to be built, and vice versa. Together, as a team, we continued to pull along, and with Jesus as the true head of our marriage and home, we began to see great change in all areas of our relationship.

Being the leader that others want to follow is truly an inside job. Jesus had a pure heart and unfailing character. The more you surrender your heart, your wants, your will, and your desires to Him, the more others will want to follow you. The more you surrender to His leadership and His top cover, the more your wife will respect you and want to come alongside you to help execute the vision that Jesus has for you and your marriage.

DISCUSSION QUESTIONS

1. How can we provide top cover for each other in our marriage, shielding one another from unnecessary stress, challenges, or external pressures?

2. In what areas of our marriage or family life do you feel you need more top cover, and how can I better provide that protection for you?

3. How can we proactively identify potential "threats" to our marriage and provide top cover for each other before these challenges cause harm?

PRAYER

Heavenly Father, we thank You for being our ultimate source of protection and guidance. Just as You cover us with Your love and strength, we ask for Your help as we seek to provide "top cover" in our marriage—guarding, shielding, and uplifting each other as we walk through life together.

Lord, remind us that marriage is a sacred covenant, where each of us is called to be a shelter for the other. Teach us to be sensitive to each other's needs and to protect our union from anything that would seek to divide or harm us. May we always be willing to step in with love and understanding, providing comfort and strength when the other needs it most. Just as You watch over our coming and going, help us to watch over each other with care, patience, and a heart committed to unity.

We pray, Father, for the wisdom to provide spiritual, emotional, and physical support. When one of us is facing struggles or doubts, let the other be a source of encouragement and resilience. May we each find strength in knowing that we are never alone and that we are protected under Your divine covering. Teach us to bring peace into our relationship, to act with selflessness, and to create a safe place where love can flourish.

Lord, thank You for this sacred responsibility and for the promise of Your presence in our marriage. Help us to reflect Your protective love in all that we do, keeping our bond strong and our hearts focused on You.

In Jesus' name, we pray. Amen.

Chapter 11
UNIFIED ADVANCEMENT

When Kristina and I were at our lowest point, I described our love as a glacier—once strong, resilient, and able to withstand any weather conditions. But over time, that glacier had cracked and separated, seemingly beyond repair. We had grown apart, and what was once a unified "us" had split into two separate beings. Sadly, this is a common scenario for many couples we've counseled. They stop moving forward together and start drifting in different directions.

In the military, growth is expected, honored, and recognized. Promotion is a major achievement and a nod to our commitment and leadership capabilities. As we climb the ranks, these promotions become increasingly meaningful. They are always celebrated among our brothers and sisters in arms, with pinning ceremonies that uphold long-standing protocols and traditions. During these ceremonies, we take a moment to thank those who have helped us along the way. We acknowledge that our growth and promotion did not happen in isolation but with the support of our comrades, families, and spouses.

In marriage, we must be intentional about growing together. Even if you have grown apart, like Kristina and I did, you can decide to grow back together. The first step is to make decisions based on faith rather than emotion. Emotions are real, but our decisions should be grounded in the Bible and what God says. In moments of tension, it's crucial to pause and not make any major life decisions based on fleeting feelings. Invite God into the conversation. I can't stress this enough: When you ask God to come into the midst of your relationship, it enables you to recalibrate, repent, and move together in one direction.

Psalm 133:1 (NKJV) beautifully states, "Behold, how good and how pleasant *it is* for brethren to dwell together in unity!" This is where the blessing comes from as we see in verse 3 of that same chapter ("for there the Lord commanded the blessing, Life forevermore"). Growing together in your relationship with Jesus is the most important thing you can do as a couple. Only God can meet your deepest needs. As you pray and attend church together, you grow in your partnership. This spiritual unity nurtures a deep emotional and physical bond, making your relationship resilient and strong.

In the military, we understand the importance of unity and teamwork. Each member of the unit plays a crucial role, and success depends on everyone working together towards a common goal. This same principle applies to marriage. Just as soldiers train together, fight together, and live together to create a bond that transcends individual differences, couples must cultivate a deep sense of unity. This unity is critical for mission success.

By growing together intentionally and inviting God into our relationships, you can move forward as a united front, fulfilling our God-given roles and responsibilities with grace and strength.

I would love to share with you a prayer that Kristina and I have been praying together for years. May this help you as you strive to achieve unity in your marriages:

Father, I come to You now in the mighty name of Jesus. I ask for Your hand of protection over our marriage. We confess, Lord, that we have grown apart, and we seek Your forgiveness for where we have failed in this area. Set us free from past hurts and unrealistic expectations. Come into our midst, Lord, and bring us back into union. We invite You into every conversation we have. Unite us, Lord, in a bond of friendship and understanding. Help us to keep You at the forefront of our lives and remind us of the reasons we fell in love. We thank You in advance for this victory. In Jesus' name, Amen.

By embracing these principles and seeking God's guidance, we can rebuild and strengthen our marriages, just as Kristina and I did, transforming what seemed like a broken glacier into a strong, unified force.

DISCUSSION QUESTIONS

1. In what ways do you feel we have grown together as a couple, and how can we continue to intentionally grow together in the next season of our marriage?

2. How can we encourage each other's personal growth—emotionally, spiritually, and professionally—while ensuring that we are still growing together as a couple?

3. What are some practical ways we can intentionally grow together in our faith, communication, and intimacy, ensuring our marriage continues to thrive even through challenges?

PRAYER

Father, I come to You now in the mighty name of Jesus. I ask for Your hand of protection over our marriage. We confess, Lord, that we have grown apart, and we seek Your forgiveness for where we have failed in this area. Set us free from past hurts and unrealistic expectations. Come into our midst, Lord, and bring us back into union. We invite You into every conversation we have. Unite us, Lord, in a bond of friendship and understanding. Help us to keep You at the forefront of our lives and remind us of the reasons we fell in love. We thank You in advance for this victory. In Jesus' name, Amen.

Chapter 12
ASSET MANAGEMENT

In the Bible, there are roughly 2,350 verses about money—more than double the number about faith and prayer combined. Jesus frequently addressed money, discussing it in about 15 percent of His sermons and 16 of His 38 parables.[1] This emphasis shows how important God considers financial matters. We learn that we are not owners but stewards of everything we have.

In the military, asset management involves strategically handling resources like finances, equipment, personnel, and supplies to ensure mission readiness and operational efficiency. Having the right resources at the right time is crucial for the success of military operations. Similarly, asset management within a relationship ensures the health and growth of the union. In our marriage, financial management was a major source of stress due to a lack of transparency. One of us controlled all spending without communicating where the money went, leading to living paycheck to paycheck—not from a lack of resources but from poor management. Understanding each other's financial language was key to addressing this.

[1] Envoy Financial, "Bible Verses About Money and Stewardship," accessed November 1, 2024, https://www.envoyfinancial.com/bible-verses-about-money-and-stewardship/#:~:-text=Did%20you%20know%20that%20there,related%20to%20money%20and%20possessions

For both Kristina and myself, finances represent success and security; however, for Kristina, they also represent love. Spending money was my wife's way of expressing love for me and our son, and when we disagreed about finances, Kristina felt unloved,. This difference in perspective created tension and misunderstandings. Once we understood how finances affected each of us, we were able to approach the subject more empathetically.

Military life is unpredictable, with income and expenses fluctuating due to deployments, relocations, and unexpected orders. Navigating finances together helps us face these uncertainties. Setting up an emergency fund, planning for relocations, and understanding military benefits are essential for financial security.

When one spouse is deployed, the other often handles the finances alone. Clear communication and shared financial goals are vital. Creating a joint budget and regularly discussing financial goals keep both partners on the same page, building trust and unity.

Making informed decisions about spending, saving, and investing involves practicing stewardship by using resources wisely as gifts from God. This includes thoughtful spending, charitable giving, and planning for the future, with a focus on tithing and donations to support your community. Debt management is essential to avoid impulsive financial decisions, and you need a clear plan to pay off debts and live within your means. Investing in education and career development, plus utilizing benefits like the GI Bill and spouse education programs, can enhance a family's financial future. Additionally, understanding and regularly reviewing insurance and retirement plans helps to ensure long-term security and adaptation to changing circumstances.

Financial management is crucial for military marriages, as it provides stability, security, and alignment with Christian values. By planning wisely, communicating openly, and seeking God's guidance, military couples can navigate financial challenges and build a strong, resilient partnership. This journey involves recognizing that our resources are blessings from God and managing them with care and respect. It's about working together, understanding each other's perspectives, and supporting each other through the unique challenges of military life.

DISCUSSION QUESTIONS

1. How can we ensure that we manage our finances in a way that reflects our shared priorities and long-term goals as a couple?

2. What are some areas of our financial life where we can improve communication about budgeting, spending, and saving?

3. How can we work together to create a financial plan that ensures stability and prepares us for potential future challenges, such as deployments, relocations, or changes in income?

PRAYER

Heavenly Father, we come before You with gratitude for the many blessings You have entrusted to us. Thank You for the gift of our marriage, and for the resources, time, and talents You've given us to steward together. We recognize that all we have comes from You, and we ask for Your guidance as we manage these blessings wisely and purposefully.

Lord, teach us to be faithful stewards of our finances, using them in ways that honor You and build a secure foundation for our family. Help us to approach every decision with wisdom, keeping generosity, prudence, and unity at the center of our plans. May we seek Your counsel in how we save, spend, and give, so that we can be a blessing to each other and to those around us.

We ask for Your help in managing our time and energy, knowing that these, too, are precious resources. Show us how to prioritize our marriage, to invest in our relationship, and to make time for the moments that nurture our bond. Remind us to cherish the days we share, to build each other up, and to keep our hearts aligned with Your purpose for our lives.

Father, may we also be good stewards of the talents and abilities You have placed in us. Help us to use our unique strengths to serve one another and to fulfill the calling You have set before us. Let us encourage each other's gifts and honor the ways You have made us to complement one another.

Thank You, Lord, for entrusting us with these blessings. May we always be mindful of Your provision and strive to manage each asset with gratitude, integrity, and love. In Jesus' name, we pray. Amen.

Chapter 13
INTEGRITY FIRST

In the military, "integrity first" is one of our core values. It underscores the importance of honesty, accountability, and moral courage. These principles are essential not only for achieving mission success but also for ensuring the trust and cohesion necessary for effective operations. This same unwavering commitment to integrity is crucial in marriage, where transparency and trust form the bedrock of a strong and healthy relationship.

The biblical story of Adam and Eve, who were both naked and unashamed, serves as a powerful illustration of transparency and purity. This state of openness is what we should strive for in our marriages. When spouses are completely honest and vulnerable with each other, there are no secrets or hidden agendas—just pure, unadulterated openness and intimacy.

Maintaining integrity in both military service and marriage requires a continuous commitment. In the military, this might involve being truthful in reports, owning up to mistakes, and consistently acting with honor. In marriage, it means being open about finances, discussing challenges and aspirations, and staying faithful in every aspect of the relationship. This ongoing dedication to integrity ensures that trust is upheld and the relationship remains strong.

Integrity was an issue for Kristina and me because we both felt we could not be fully transparent with one another out of fear of how the other would respond. We finally realized that being honest took such a weight off both our shoulders. While I could not control how Kristina responded, I could control how I dealt with her response. This breakthrough helped us understand that true intimacy in marriage is built on a foundation of trust and openness.

In the military, integrity involves doing the right thing, even when no one is watching. This means being truthful, adhering to ethical standards, and taking responsibility for one's actions. A lapse in integrity can lead to serious consequences, including loss of trust, compromised security, and mission failure. The trust and reliability built through integrity are crucial for the success of military operations and the safety of service members.

Similarly, in marriage, integrity is about maintaining honesty, fidelity, and transparency with one's spouse. When integrity is compromised, it can lead to breaches of trust and emotional disconnect. Just as a lack of integrity can jeopardize a military mission, it can also undermine the foundation of a marriage. Concealing or being deceitful about important aspects of one's life can create a rift that is difficult to repair, leading to misunderstandings and a weakening of the marital bond.

Whether in the military or in a marriage, upholding integrity is essential for maintaining strong, resilient partnerships. It reflects our commitment to Christian values and our dedication to living a life of honesty and moral courage.

DISCUSSION QUESTIONS

1. In what areas of our marriage can we strengthen our commitment to integrity, and how can we hold each other accountable to honesty and transparency?

2. How do we navigate difficult situations in a way that ensures we remain true to our values and principles, even when making the right choice is challenging?

3. What steps can we take to ensure that we are always open and honest with each other, especially in uncomfortable or difficult circumstances?

PRAYER

Heavenly Father, we thank You for the gift of marriage and the sacred bond we share. We ask for Your guidance and strength to build our relationship on the foundation of integrity. Teach us to honor each other with honesty, faithfulness, and unwavering commitment, so that our marriage reflects Your love and truth.

Lord, help us to put integrity first in all we do, choosing to act with transparency, respect, and trustworthiness. Let our words be truthful, our intentions pure, and our actions aligned with Your will. When we face temptations or challenges, give us the strength to stand firm and to protect our marriage with integrity and faithfulness.

Remind us that integrity isn't just about avoiding wrongdoing, but about intentionally building a marriage that honors You. May we treat each other with respect, keep our promises, and stay true to the vows we made. Help us to be quick to forgive, slow to anger, and willing to admit when we fall short, so that we can grow stronger together.

Lord, may our marriage be a testament to Your grace, a relationship that reflects integrity in every aspect. Guide us to live in a way that brings honor to You, knowing that as we walk in integrity, our love will deepen and our bond will be strengthened. Thank You for being our example and for giving us the wisdom to uphold these values.

In Jesus' name, we pray. Amen.

Chapter 14
RULES OF ENGAGEMENT

Rules of Engagement (ROE) are designed to maintain order, discipline, and ethical standards during engagements. They ensure that actions taken are lawful, appropriate, and strategically sound. Similarly, in a marriage, following these principles helps create a framework for resolving conflicts effectively and respectfully.

Authorization and Command: In the military, ROE are set by higher command structures, outlining who has the authority to initiate engagements. In marriage, this can be paralleled by mutual agreement on when and how to address conflicts. It's important for both partners to feel empowered to initiate difficult conversations, ensuring that issues are addressed in a timely and mutually respectful manner. For example, I do not like discussing major issues in the evening. Kristina and I agreed that if there were issues we needed to discuss, we would set a time to address them when we were both fresh.

Self-Defense: ROE emphasize the right to self-defense, allowing personnel to protect themselves and others from immediate threats. In marriage, this means protecting oneself emotionally and mentally during conflicts. It was never *what* Kristina said, but *how* she said it that deeply impacted my responses to tense situations. Establishing boundaries and ensuring that both partners feel safe to express their feelings without fear of attack is crucial.

Proportionality: Military ROE require that the use of force be proportional to the threat. In marital conflicts, this principle encourages addressing issues fairly and without overreaction. It's about staying focused on the present issue and dealing with it in a balanced manner, preventing the escalation of minor disagreements into major disputes. Sometimes you have to take a breather and revisit issues later when emotions are calmer.

Discrimination: This principle involves distinguishing between combatants and non-combatants, ensuring protection for non-combatants. In marriage, it translates to focusing on the specific issue at hand rather than attacking the person. It's crucial to separate the problem from the partner and avoid personal attacks. When Kristina reminded me we are on the same team, it would completely change the trajectory of the situation.

Necessity: The ROE stipulate that force should only be used when absolutely necessary. Similarly, conflicts in marriage should be addressed thoughtfully and only when necessary. Avoiding unnecessary arguments over trivial issues helps maintain harmony and focus on what truly matters. We had to learn that "my way" wasn't the only way. The way I fold laundry may not be Kristina's way, but the clothes were folded, and she knew that my heart was to be helpful.

De-escalation: ROE encourage de-escalating situations to prevent unnecessary violence. In marriage, de-escalation means recognizing when a conflict is getting out of hand and taking steps to calm things down. Taking breaks to cool off or agreeing to revisit the conversation later can prevent escalation and lead to more productive discussions. Just be sure to set a time to revisit the conversation.

Accountability: Military personnel must account for their actions. In marriage, this involves taking responsibility for one's actions and words, being willing to apologize, and working towards reconciliation. Accountability builds trust and shows commitment to the relationship.

Clear Communication: ROE emphasize the importance of clear communication. In marriage, partners need to understand and respect each other's perspectives. It helps prevent misunderstandings and keeps the focus on resolving the issue at hand.

Applying ROE principles helps create a structured and respectful approach to conflict resolution, ensuring both partners feel heard and valued. Kristina and I now approach difficult situations with the mindset of fighting fair with love. We ask ourselves, "How can we both win?" It's about creating an environment where both partners can express themselves openly and honestly, without fear of retribution or escalation. This leads to a healthier, more resilient marriage.

As Proverbs 15:1 reminds us, "A soft answer turns away wrath, but a harsh word stirs up anger" (NKJV). By embracing these principles and seeking God's guidance, we can navigate the complexities of both military life and marriage with grace and strength.

DISCUSSION QUESTIONS

1. What "rules of engagement" should we establish for handling conflict in our marriage?

2. How can we honor our agreed-upon rules of engagement, especially during high-stress situations or times when we're feeling emotionally charged?

3. How can we use the rules of engagement not just to manage conflict but also to strengthen communication and trust within our marriage?

PRAYER

Heavenly Father, we come before You, grateful for the bond of marriage and the privilege of sharing life together. We ask for Your guidance in establishing and honoring our "rules of engagement"—principles that lead us to communicate, love, and serve each other in ways that honor You.

Lord, teach us to approach each interaction with patience, respect, and understanding. Help us to listen more than we speak, to respond with grace rather than react out of anger, and to always seek unity over division. May we remember that our words have power, and let them be used to build each other up and bring healing, even in moments of disagreement.

Give us wisdom to resolve conflict with humility, valuing each other's perspectives and seeking solutions that strengthen our relationship. When we face challenges, remind us that we are a team, united in purpose and love. Show us how to set healthy boundaries that protect our marriage and to engage in ways that bring peace, clarity, and compassion.

Father, may our "rules of engagement" reflect Your love and truth. Help us to communicate with honesty and kindness, to forgive each other fully, and to strive for harmony in all that we do. Guide us to handle every situation with integrity, so that our marriage becomes a testimony of Your grace and goodness.

In Jesus' name, we pray. Amen.

Chapter 15
BAND OF BROTHERS

Everyday intimacy is the cornerstone of both military life and marriage as it creates the deep connections and trust essential for overcoming life's many challenges. Reflecting on my own experiences and favorite sources of inspiration, I often turn to the series *Band of Brothers*. The profound emotional bonds among the men of Easy Company are striking, and Major Dick Winters, my favorite officer, exemplifies this through his unwavering support, empathy, and dedication to his men. Facing the horrors of war together, these men form bonds that go beyond mere camaraderie—they become a family. This powerful illustration of emotional intimacy is built on shared experiences, trust, and mutual respect.

Major Winters' leadership style is deeply rooted in emotional intelligence. He understands the importance of connecting with his men on a personal level, acknowledging their fears, and providing the emotional support they need to persevere. His ability to empathize with his soldiers, offer words of encouragement, and lead by example advances a sense of security and trust that is essential for their collective resilience. This same principle applies to marriage, especially within the unique dynamics of military life.

The frequent deployments, relocations, and inherent dangers of military life require a strong foundation of emotional intimacy. Just as Major Winters communicated openly with his men, ensuring they felt heard and understood, couples must prioritize transparent dialogue to build trust and deepen their emotional bond. This level of openness can be challenging, especially during prolonged separations, but it is essential for maintaining a strong connection.

In my own marriage with Kristina, we faced our share of challenges regarding intimacy. Kristina is very affectionate, whereas I am not naturally inclined that way. I mistakenly believed that because we were physically intimate, we were meeting all our intimacy needs. However, intimacy goes far beyond physical interaction. I learned this lesson through a conversation with a colleague who explained intimacy using the framework of Comprehensive Airman Fitness (CAF), a program we all know in the military. CAF includes four aspects, one of them being social/emotional, which focuses on the need for connectedness. This made me realize that intimacy is for everyone and is a vital part of our well-being, so much so that our military has established a program to emphasize its importance.

Mutual support is another crucial element. In *Band of Brothers,* soldiers support each other unconditionally, creating unity that helps them endure hardships. Similarly, in marriage, partners must offer each other unwavering support, being present both physically and emotionally. This reinforces the intimacy that sustains the relationship.

A Scripture passage that beautifully encapsulates the importance of intimacy is Ecclesiastes 4:9–10: "Two *are* better than one ... If either of them falls down, one can help the other up." These words highlight the importance of partnership and mutual support, which are vital for both military life and marriage. Prioritizing emotional intimacy helps couples build a strong, enduring relationship that thrives even in adversity.

Kristina and I have come a long way in understanding and nurturing intimacy in our marriage. By prioritizing open communication, offering mutual support, and recognizing the importance of emotional connectedness, we have built a deeper, more resilient relationship. For military couples facing similar struggles, embracing these principles can help you navigate the unique challenges of military life while building a strong foundation of trust and love in your marriage.

DISCUSSION QUESTIONS

1. How can we build and maintain emotional intimacy in our marriage, especially during difficult times or long separations?

2. What are some ways we can cultivate a deeper level of trust and emotional connection in our marriage, ensuring that we both feel supported and understood?

3. Emotional intimacy is not only about sharing victories but also about standing together in times of loss and hardship. How can we ensure that we are emotionally available to each other, especially in moments of stress or hardship?

PRAYER

Heavenly Father, we thank You for the gift of marriage and the powerful bond we share as husband and wife. Just as soldiers become a "Band of Brothers," bound by loyalty and united in purpose, we ask that You strengthen our unity and deepen our commitment to one another. Help us to stand together, supporting and protecting each other in all seasons of life.

Lord, teach us to walk in loyalty, to honor our commitment, and to remain steadfast even when times are challenging. May our marriage be built on trust and faithfulness, as we rely on You to be the foundation of our relationship. Remind us that we are not alone, but joined together by Your love and strengthened by Your presence.

In moments of struggle, help us to remember that we are a team, standing side by side, just as brothers and sisters in arms. Give us the courage to face life's battles together, knowing that our strength comes from You. Let our unity and love be a testimony to others, reflecting the strength and resilience You desire for us.

Thank You, Lord, for being our ultimate source of strength and protection. May our marriage reflect the loyalty, trust, and unity of a true "band of brothers," committed to standing by each other, come what may.

In Jesus' name, we pray. Amen.

Chapter 16

A SACRED BOND

Sexual intimacy is a critical component of marriage, especially in the context of military life, where unique challenges can put significant strain on relationships. A 2015 study by Walden University found that "around 70% of wives of deployed servicemen believe that their husbands had been unfaithful while on duty."[2] Two years later, another study found that "across the deployment period, the prevalence of sexual infidelity was strikingly high (22.6%) compared with the annual community estimates (1.5%–4%)."[3]

Kristina and I were married in Korea while I was on a remote assignment. When I returned home, we had a vow renewal ceremony for our family. During our premarital counseling, our pastor took us to the church basement and gave us some unconventional advice: "Sex is not everything. It is not that important, and if you don't have it often, it is okay. God made sex for us to have children, but there is more to marriage than sex." While there is some truth in the idea that marriage

[2] SOFREP News Team, "Infidelity In Military Marriages May Be More Common Than You Think," SOFREP Miliary Grade Content, May, 23, 2023, https://sofrep.com/entertainment/infidelity-military-marriage; See also https://scholarworks.waldenu.edu/cgi/viewcontent.cgi?article=1757&context=dissertations

[3] Christina Balderrama-Durbin et al., "The Risk for Marital Infidelity across a Year-Long Deployment.," Journal of Family Psychology 31, no. 5 (August 2017): 629–34, https://doi.org/10.1037/fam0000281.

encompasses more than just physical intimacy, it is crucial to acknowledge that sexual intimacy plays a significant role in a healthy, fulfilling marriage.

God created sex as a powerful force that binds a husband and wife together. It is a unique aspect of marriage that cannot be shared with anyone else. Just as battle buddies and wingmen form sacred bonds through shared experiences and mutual trust, so too must husbands and wives nurture their sexual intimacy to maintain a strong connection.

The apostle Paul's words in 1 Corinthians 7:3–6 resonate deeply with this concept:

> Let the husband render to his wife the affection due her, and likewise also the wife to her husband. The wife does not have authority over her own body, but the husband *does*. And likewise, the husband does not have authority over his own body, but the wife *does*. Do not deprive one another except with consent for a time, that you may give yourselves to fasting and prayer; and come together again so that Satan does not tempt you because of your lack of self-control. But I say this as a concession, not as a commandment (NKJV).

Paul emphasizes the mutual responsibility of spouses to fulfill each other's needs and the importance of coming together often. He also advises that temporary separation should be consensual and for spiritual purposes, to strengthen both partners' resolve.

We often get questions about sexual frequency in marriage. There is no one-size-fits-all rule. The objective is to come together as often as you both can. It's important to note that your desires may not always match. Kristina and I don't always want sex at the same time. In those instances, we make a concerted effort to come together regardless. Communicate your needs to one another and do everything you can to meet those needs.

Deployments and times of separation are inevitable parts of our calling, and during those periods, I encourage you, as Paul does, to spend time growing closer to the Lord. The closer you grow in your relationship with God while away, the closer you will be to your spouse when you come home. This may not be popular advice, but I can tell you firsthand that this has been true in my marriage. Maintaining sexual intimacy during seasons of forced separation can be particularly challenging, so communication is key. Regularly sharing thoughts, desires, and feelings through letters, video calls, or emails helps maintain a sense of closeness. Emotional intimacy often paves the way for sexual intimacy, even from a distance. Planning for intimate moments when together and discussing expectations beforehand can also help bridge the gap during separations.

If trust has been broken due to infidelity or other issues, rebuilding sexual intimacy requires patience, transparency, and a commitment to healing. Open communication about the hurt and the steps needed to rebuild trust is essential. Both partners must be willing to work on the relationship, seeking professional counseling if necessary. Re-establishing emotional intimacy is a critical step towards restoring sexual intimacy.

The high rate of infidelity in military marriages highlights the need for proactive measures to protect and nurture the marital bond. Just as soldiers rely on their battle buddies and wingmen for support and accountability, military couples must rely on each other, prioritizing their relationship and safeguarding it against the temptations and stressors that come with military life.

Kristina and I learned the importance of prioritizing our sexual intimacy despite the challenges. While sex is not the entirety of marriage, it is a vital component that strengthens our bond and enhances our connection. By understanding each other's needs and making intentional efforts to maintain intimacy, we can build a resilient and fulfilling marriage.

DISCUSSION QUESTIONS

1. How can we ensure that our sexual intimacy reflects the emotional and spiritual connection we share?

2. In what ways can we protect the sacredness of our sexual intimacy from external pressures or distractions that may arise in our busy military life?

3. How can we communicate openly and lovingly about our needs, desires, and boundaries so that the sexual aspect of our relationship continues to grow and flourish?

PRAYER

Heavenly Father, we thank You for the gift of intimacy in marriage, a beautiful reflection of the love and unity You designed for us. We ask that You bless our physical relationship, deepening our connection and strengthening the bond we share as husband and wife. Teach us to approach each other with love, respect, and a heart that desires to serve, honoring this special part of our relationship as a sacred and joyful gift.

Lord, help us to cultivate a sense of openness, vulnerability, and trust in our intimacy. Remove any barriers that keep us from fully giving and receiving love, and help us to communicate openly, sharing our desires, needs, and emotions with honesty and kindness. Let our physical connection be a source of joy, comfort, and renewal, reminding us of the covenant we made and the love that brought us together.

May our intimacy draw us closer, not only to each other but to You, knowing that You are present in every aspect of our marriage. Teach us to cherish these moments together, to approach each other with tenderness and grace, and to keep our love alive and thriving. We thank You, Lord, for this gift and ask that You guide us to honor it in a way that brings us closer to each other and glorifies You.

In Jesus' name, we pray. Amen.

CONCLUSION

This project was born out of one of the darkest and most challenging seasons of our marriage. We were at the edge, facing a level of brokenness we never thought possible. Our marriage felt dead, and we didn't see a way forward. But God stepped into our story in a way that only He could. He took what was shattered and breathed new life into it, performing a miracle that transformed us from the inside out. Today, we stand on the other side of that tragedy, and we can truly say we are healthier, happier, and more deeply in love than ever before. We look at each other now with gratitude, knowing that our love was not only restored but renewed. Fighting for our marriage was the best decision we ever made. And if God did this for us, He can do it for you too. He wants that healing, that joy, and that strength for every marriage willing to turn to Him.

Marriage is more than just a relationship; it's a mission. It's one of the greatest missions you'll ever receive. The choice to accept that mission is yours, and if you choose to embrace it with God at the center, you'll find a life of adventure, stability, and purpose. The journey isn't always easy, but the rewards are profound. When we commit to doing marriage God's way—honoring each other, living with integrity, and growing together in faith—we set a course that leads to blessings not only for ourselves but for those around us.

Your marriage has the potential to be a blessing to others and to impact generations to come. When you choose to serve and love your spouse selflessly, you create a legacy that echoes beyond your own family. Others will see the strength of your bond, and they'll be encouraged by it. Your children and their children will look back on your example of faithfulness, resilience, and commitment, and they'll be inspired to pursue the same in their lives.

For those of us who serve in the military, a strong marriage is one of the most rewarding foundations we can have. It not only supports our mission but also strengthens our resolve, giving us the stability to face whatever comes our way. A marriage done God's way can become a source of strength that impacts the very fabric of our nation. When we hold fast to each other and lean on God's guidance, we become living examples of hope and resilience. And in a world that often feels uncertain, a marriage grounded in faith can be a powerful witness of God's enduring love and strength.

As we conclude this journey with you, we want to thank you for walking alongside us. Sharing our story and what we've learned has been an honor, and we hope it's been as meaningful to you as it has been to us. If you're facing your own struggles or wondering if your marriage can be restored, remember this: God is in the business of redemption. He can breathe life into what feels dead, just as He did for us. Embrace the mission of marriage with open hearts, trust in His ways, and allow Him to work in you. You'll find a life richer than you could have imagined—a life of purpose, love, and adventure that is secure and unbreakable.

God has amazing things in store for you and your marriage. As you go forward, may you experience the fullness of His blessings, and may your relationship become a light for others to follow. Thank you for being a part of this journey with us.

ABOUT THE AUTHORS

Chaplain, Major Matthew Spencer and Kristina Spencer bring over 20 years of combined experience in ministry, counseling, and leadership to their work with military couples and families. Matt, a USAF Chaplain with a background in Security Forces, provides pastoral care, spiritual growth opportunities, and worship leadership to Airmen and their families, leveraging his extensive service across enlisted and officer roles worldwide. Kristina, an ordained minister, XO Marriage content writer, and certified marriage mediator, has led impactful women's ministries, young adult groups, and large-scale events while mentoring others in their faith and relationships. Together, they are passionate about equipping couples with practical strategies and biblical principles to build resilient, God-centered marriages, inspiring hope and transformation through their personal and professional experiences.

NOTES